SELLING MANHATTAN

Also by Carol Ann Duffy

STANDING FEMALE NUDE
THE OTHER COUNTRY
MEAN TIME
SELECTED POEMS

Anthologies

I WOULDN'T THANK YOU FOR A VALENTINE
ANVIL NEW POETS 2
STOPPING FOR DEATH

Carol Ann Duffy

SELLING
MANHATTAN

ANVIL PRESS POETRY

First published in 1987
by Anvil Press Poetry Ltd
Neptune House 70 Royal Hill London SE10 8RF

Reprinted in 1989, 1990, 1992
New edition 1996
Reprinted in 1998

ISBN 0 85646 295 0

This book is published
with financial assistance from
The Arts Council of England

Set in Monotype Plantin Light by Anvil
Printed in Great Britain
at the Arc & Throstle Press, Todmorden, Lancs

A catalogue record for this book
is available from the British Library

FOR LIZZIE

ACKNOWLEDGEMENTS

Some of these poems have been previously published in *The Poetry Book Society Anthology 1986/87, Thrown Voices* (Turret Books), *Ambit, Aurora, New Statesman, The North, Outposts, Poetry Matters, Poetry Review, The Rialto, Slightly Soiled, Stand.* Acknowledgement is due to *Touch the Earth, a self-portrait of Indian existence,* ed. T. C. McLuhan (1972), for material used in the title poem.

CONTENTS

PRACTISING BEING DEAD

Your own ghost, you stand in dark rain
and light aches out from the windows
to lie in pools at your feet. This is the place.
Those are the big oak doors. Behind them
a waxed floor stretches away, backwards
down a corridor of years. The trees sigh.
You are both watching and remembering. Neither.

Inside, the past is the scent of candles the moment
they go out. You saw her, ancient and yellow,
laid out inside that alcove at the stairhead,
a broken string of water on her brow.
For weeks the game was Practising Being Dead,
hands in the praying position, eyes closed, lips
pressed to the colour of sellotape over the breath.

It is accidental and unbearable to recall that time,
neither bitter nor sweet but gone, the future
already lost as you open door after door, each one
peeling back a sepia room empty of promise.
This evening the sky has not enough moon
to give you a shadow. Nobody hears
your footsteps walking away along the gravel drive.

DIES NATALIS

When I was cat, my mistress tossed me sweetmeats
from her couch. Even the soldiers were deferential –
she thought me sacred – I saw my sleek ghost
arch in their breastplates and I purred

my one eternal note beneath the shadow of pyramids.
The world then was measured by fine wires
which had their roots in my cat brain, trembled
for knowledge. She stroked my black pelt, singing

her different, frantic notes into my ear.
These were meanings I could not decipher. Later,
my vain, furred tongue erased a bowl of milk,
then I slept and fed on river rats...

She would throw pebbles at the soil, searching
with long, gold nails for logic in chaos;
or bathe at night in the moon's pool,
dissolving its light into wobbling pearls.

I was there, my collar of jewels and eyes shining,
my small heart impartial. Even now, at my spine's base,
the memory of a tail stirs idly, defining that night.
Cool breeze. Eucalyptus. Map of stars above

which told us nothing, randomly scattered like pebbles.
The man who feared me came at dawn, fought her
until she moaned into stillness, her ringed hand
with its pattern of death, palm up near my face.

*

Then a breath of sea air after blank decades,
my wings applauding this new shape. Far below,
the waves envied the sky, straining for blueness,
muttering in syllables of fish. I trod air, laughing,

what space was salt was safe. A speck became a ship,
filling its white sails like gulping lungs. Food swam.
I swooped, pincered the world in my beak, then soared
across the sun. The great whales lamented the past

wet years away, sending their bleak songs back
and forth between themselves. I hovered, listening,
as water slowly quenched fire. My cross on the surface
followed, marking where I was in the middle of nowhere...

Six days later found me circling the ship. Men's voices
came over the side in scraps. I warned patiently
in my private language, weighed down with loneliness.
Even the wind had dropped. The sea stood still,

flicked out its sharks, and the timber wheezed.
I could only be bird, as the wheel of the day turned slowly
between sun and moon. When night fell, it was stale,
unbearably quiet, holding the breath of the dead.

The egg was in my gut, nursing its own deaths
in a delicate shell. I remember its round weight
persistently pressing; opening my bowel onto the deck
near a young sailor, the harsh sound my cry made then.

★

But when I loved, I thought that was all I had done.
It was very ordinary, an ordinary place, the river
filthy, and with no sunset to speak of. She spoke
in a local accent, laughing at mine, kissed

with her tongue. This changed me. Christ, sweetheart,
marry me, I'll go mad. A dog barked. She ran off,
teasing, and back down the path came Happen you will...
Afterwards, because she asked, I told her my prospects,

branded her white neck. She promised herself
in exchange for a diamond ring. The sluggish water
shrugged past as we did it again. We whispered
false vows which would ruin our lives...

I cannot recall more pain. There were things one could buy
to please her, but she kept herself apart, spitefully
guarding the password. My body repelled her. Sweat.
Sinew. All that had to be hunched away in nylon sheets.

We loathed in the same dull air till silver presents came,
our two hands clasping one knife to cut a stale cake. One day,
the letter. Surgery. When the treatment did not work,
she died. I cried over the wishbone body, wondering

what was familiar, watching myself from a long way off.
I carried the remains in an urn to the allotment,
trying to remember the feel of her, but it was years,
years, and what blew back in my face was grey ash, dust.

★

Now hushed voices say I have my mother's look.
Once again, there is light. The same light. I talk
to myself in shapes, though something is constantly changing
the world, rearranging the face which stares at mine.

Most of the time I am hungry, sucking on dry air
till it gives in, turning milky and warm. Sleep
is dreamless, but when I awake I have more
to contemplate. They are trying to label me,

translate me into the right word. My small sounds
bring a bitter finger to my mouth, a taste
which cannot help or comfort me. I recall
and release in a sigh the journey here...

The man and woman are different colours and I
am both of them. These strangers own me,
pass me between them chanting my new name. They wrap
and unwrap me, a surprise they want to have again,

mouthing their tickly love to my smooth, dark flesh.
The days are mosaic, telling a story for the years
to come. I suck my thumb. New skin thickens
on my skull, to keep the moments I have lived before

locked in. I will lose my memory, learn words
which barely stretch to cover what remains unsaid. Mantras
of consolation come from those who keep my portrait
in their eyes. And when they disappear, I cry.

SANCTUARY

This morning you are not incurable, not yet, can walk
with your disease inside you, at its centre
your small pearl of hope, along the entrance path
where tall, cool pillars hold the sky. Ahead,
the archway, white, benevolent; calm doctors
who will dress you in clean robes. Now you cry
tears you have not wept for years. Relief.

Already, being here, you half believe, arriving
in Reception, acquiescent, giving your old clothes
up to the flames, giving your name. Thank you,
yes, yes, the anxious words like worry beads.
You will do as you are told, anything, accept
that the waters are holy, work wonders;
for a perfect fleshy shell exchange a golden ear.

You're sick. This placid world of thoughtful space,
philosophy, design, has taken you in. Forget.
Forget how you came here, what suffering
you endured to wait in the Circular Cure Centre
for a nurse, your heart reciting its own small number.
I want to be well, recall this treatment miles away,
pass pain on the street like a stranger. Please.

In the Library your shaking hand takes up a book,
thumbs miracles. These men were saved, prescriptions
scrawled upon their dreams. You read of venom,
oil, cream, a rooster's blood. Later your shadow
precedes you into the Chamber of Dreams. You'll dream
about yourself, chant your therapy as dawn arrives
with light for the blind stone eyes of statues.

Breathe in. Out. In. Sometimes you wake in darkness,
holding your own hand as if you will stay forever.
Think again. The months flew, that year in the Sanctuary
when you were cured. Remember a fool's face
pulling a tongue in a mirror, your dedication
carved in the Temple of Tributes. Its blatant lie
blushed on marble, one sunset as you died elsewhere.

AN OLD ATHEIST
PLACES HIS LAST BET

Ace in the hole; ten, jack, queen on the baize.
As far as I can see, you've got nothing, mate.
My old eyes are tired and it's getting late,
I have as many chips left as days.

Outside this window, a willow tree sways
in the evening breeze. Deal the cards. I wait
for a king as shadows lengthen; hesitate,
call the last bet. I think again, then raise.

Silence. I leave my card face down and stare
at the empty room. It is turning in space
slowly, sadly, and there is nothing there...

and opposite me, the dealer's vacant place
piled high with chips. We gamblers do not care,
win or lose. I turn the card, turn my poker face.

STRANGE LANGUAGE
IN NIGHT FOG

Not only the dark,
but a sudden mist also,
made where they walked an alien place.

Beasts moaned from nowhere,
the cows the moon would have,
and, to their left, the pond
had drowned itself.

They stopped,
wobbling on straight lines,
and watched the Common
playing hide-and-seek behind the fog.

A bush nipped out,
then disappeared again;
a tree stepped backwards.
Even their own hands
waved at their faces, teasing.

But it was a strange language,
spoken only yards away,
which turned the night into a dream;

although they told themselves
there must be a word for home,
if they only knew it.

I LIVE HERE NOW

I live here now, the place where the pond
was a doll's mirror and the trees were bits of twig.
I invented it, that wee dog barking
at the postman (an old soldier with one arm, still)
and the path of small grey pebbles
in the avenue of flowers. Tall daisies, buttercups.

It nearly got a prize, balanced on topsoil,
carried up to the Big Tent where grown-ups peered
over the rim of the world. *Highly Recommended.*
Being grown yourself was half a dream, warm breath
clouding the ruby tomatoes, a sudden
flash of sixpence on the bright green grass.

Come in. Take the window-seat. The clouds
are cotton wool on pipe-cleaners, cunningly placed,
which never rain. In the distance
you can see Pincushion Hill. That's me, waving,
at the top. I live here now
and sometimes wave back, over the fields, the years.

HOMESICK

When we love, when we tell ourselves we do,
we are pining for first love, somewhen,
before we thought of wanting it. When we rearrange
the rooms we end up living in, we are looking
for first light, the arrangement of light,
that time, before we knew to call it light.

Or talk of music, when we say
we cannot talk of it, but play again
C major, A flat minor, we are straining
for first sound, what we heard once,
then, in lost chords, wordless languages.

What country do we come from? This one?
The one where the sun burns
when we have night? The one
the moon chills; elsewhere, possible?

Why is our love imperfect,
music only echo of itself,
the light wrong?

We scratch in dust with sticks,
dying of homesickness
for when, where, what.

THE DUMMY

Balancing me with your hand up my back, listening
to the voice you gave me croaking for truth, you keep
me at it. Your lips don't move, but your eyes look
desperate as hell. Ask me something difficult.

Maybe we could sing together? Just teach me
the right words, I learn fast. Don't stare like that.
I'll start where you leave off. I can't tell you
anything if you don't throw me a cue line. We're dying

a death right here. Can you dance? No. I don't suppose
you'd be doing this if you could dance. Right? Why do you
keep me in that black box? I can ask questions too,
you know. I can see that worries you. Tough.

So funny things happen to everyone on the way to most places.
Come on. You can do getter than that, can't you?

MODEL VILLAGE

See the cows placed just so on the green hill.
Cows say *Moo.* The sheep look like little clouds,
don't they? Sheep say Baa. Grass is green
and the pillar-box is red. Wouldn't it be strange
if grass were red? This is the graveyard
where the villagers bury their dead. Miss Maiden
lives opposite in her cottage. She has a cat.
The cat says *Miaow.* What does Miss Maiden say?

I poisoned her, but no one knows. Mother, I said,
drink your tea. Arsenic. Four sugars. He waited
years for me, but she had more patience. One day,
he didn't come back. I looked in the mirror,
saw her grey hair, her lips of reproach. I found
the idea in a paperback. I loved him, you see,
who never so much as laid a finger. Perhaps now
you've learnt your lesson, she said, pouring
another cup. Yes, Mother, yes. Drink it all up.

The white fence around the farmyard
looks as though it's smiling. The hens are tidying
the yard. Hens say *Cluck* and give us eggs. Pigs
are pink and give us sausages. *Grunt,* they say.
Wouldn't it be strange if hens laid sausages?
Hee-haw, says the donkey. The farmhouse
is yellow and shines brightly in the sun. Notice
the horse. Horses say *Neigh.* What does the Farmer say?

To tell the truth, it haunts me. I'm a simple man,
not given to fancy. The flock was ahead of me,
the dog doing his job like a good 'un. Then
I saw it. Even the animals stiffened in fright. Look,
I understand the earth, treat death and birth
the same. A fistful of soil tells me plainly
what I need to know. You plant, you grow, you reap.
But since then, sleep has been difficult. When I shovel
deep down, I'm searching for something. Digging, desperately.

There's the church and there's the steeple.
Open the door and there are the people. Pigeons
roost in the church roof. Pigeons say *Coo*.
The church bells say *Ding-dong*, calling
the faithful to worship. What God says
can be read in the Bible. See the postman's dog
waiting patiently outside church. *Woof*, he says.
Amen, say the congregation. What does Vicar say?

Now they have all gone, I shall dress up
as a choirboy. I have shaved my legs. How smooth
they look. Smooth, pink knees. If I am not good,
I shall deserve punishment. Perhaps the choirmistress
will catch me smoking behind the organ. A good boy
would own up. I am naughty. I can feel
the naughtiness under my smock. Smooth, pink naughtiness.
The choirmistress shall wear boots and put me
over her lap. I tremble and dissolve into childhood.

Quack, say the ducks on the village pond. Did you
see the frog? Frogs say *Croak*. The village-folk shop
at the butcher's, the baker's, the candlestick maker's.
The Grocer has a parrot. Parrots say *Pretty Polly*
and *Who's a pretty boy then?* The Vicar is nervous
of parrots, isn't he? Miss Maiden is nervous
of Vicar and the Farmer is nervous of everything.
The library clock says *Tick-tock*. What does the Librarian say?

Ssssh. I've seen them come and go over the years,
my ears tuned for every whisper. This place
is a refuge, the volumes breathing calmly
on their still shelves. I glide between them
like a doctor on his rounds, know their cases. Tomes
do no harm, here I'm safe. Outside is chaos,
lives with no sense of plot. Behind each front door
lurks truth, danger. I peddle fiction. Believe
you me, the books in everyone's head are stranger...

THE BRINK OF SHRIEKS

for S. B.

Don't ask me how, but I've fetched up
living with him. You can laugh. It's no joke
from where I'm sitting. Up to the back teeth.

That *walk*. You feel ashamed going out. So-and-so's
method of perambulation, he calls it. My arse.
Thank God for plastic hips. He'll be queueing.

And the *language*. What can you say? Nothing.
Those wee stones make me want to brain him,
so they do. They're only the tip of the iceberg.

Time who stopped? says I. Ash-grey vests,
you try cleaning them. Heartbreaking. Too many nights
lying in yon ditch, counting. God's truth, I *boil*.

See him, he's not uttered a peep in weeks.
And me? I'm on the brink of shrieks.

RECOGNITION

Things get away from one.
I've let myself go, I know.
Children? I've had three
and don't even know them.

I strain to remember a time
when my body felt lighter.
Years. My face is swollen
with regrets. I put powder on,

but it flakes off. I love him,
through habit, but the proof
has evaporated. He gets upset.
I tried to do all the essentials

on one trip. Foolish, yes,
but I was weepy all morning.
Quiche. A blond boy swung me up
in his arms and promised the earth.

You see, this came back to me
as I stood on the scales.
I wept. Shallots. In the window,
creamy ladies held a pose

which left me clogged and old.
The waste. I'd forgotten my purse,
fumbled; the shopgirl gaped at me,
compassionless. Claret. I blushed.

Cheese. Kleenex. *It did happen.*
I lay in my slip on wet grass,
laughing. Years. I had to rush out,
blind in a hot flush, and bumped

into an anxious, dowdy matron
who touched the cold mirror
and stared at me. Stared
and said I'm sorry sorry sorry.

ABSOLUTELY

Thank you. Yes please. After you. Don't mind
my asking this, but is politeness strange?
Don't mention it. What do you think yourself?

The politeness of strangers worries me,
like surgical gloves. Irrational, I know.
Nasties in childhood or the woodshed.

How very interesting. Magritte opened the door
to a journalist, politely bowed him in, then
booted him up the arse right across the room.

AND HOW ARE WE TODAY?

The little people in the radio are picking on me
again. It is sunny, but they are going to make it
rain. I do not like their voices, they have voices
like cold tea with skin on. I go O O O.

The flowers are plastic. There is all dust
on the petals. I go Ugh. Real flowers die,
but at least they are a comfort to us all.
I know them by name, listen. Rose. Tulip. Lily.

I live inside someone else's head. He hears me
with his stethoscope, so it is no use
sneaking home at five o'clock to his nice house
because I am in his ear going Breathe Breathe.

I might take my eye out and swallow it
to bring some attention to myself. Winston did.
His name was in the paper. For the time being
I make noises to annoy them and then I go BASTARDS.

PSYCHOPATH

I run my metal comb through the D.A. and pose
my reflection between dummies in the window at Burton's.
Lamp light. Jimmy Dean. All over town, ducking and diving,
my shoes scud sparks against the night. She is in the canal.
Let me make myself crystal. With a good-looking girl crackling
in four petticoats, you feel like a king. She rode past me
on a wooden horse, laughing, and the air sang *Johnny,*
Remember Me. I turned the world faster, flash.

I don't talk much. I swing up beside them and do it
with my eyes. Brando. She was clean. I could smell her.
I thought, Here we go, old son. The fairground spun round us
and she blushed like candyfloss. You can woo them
with goldfish and coconuts, whispers in the Tunnel of Love.
When I zip up the leather, I'm in a new skin, I touch it
and love myself, sighing Some little lady's going to get lucky
tonight. My breath wipes me from the looking-glass.

We move from place to place. We leave on the last morning
with the scent of local girls on our fingers. They wear
our lovebites on their necks. I know what women want,
a handrail to Venus. She said *Please* and *Thank you*
to the toffee-apple, teddy-bear. I thought I was on, no error.
She squealed on the dodgems, clinging to my leather sleeve.
I took a swig of whisky from the flask and frenched it
down her throat. *No*, she said, *Don't*, like they always do.

Dirty Alice flicked my dick out when I was twelve.
She jeered. I nicked a quid and took her to the spinney.
I remember the wasps, the sun blazing as I pulled
her knickers down. I touched her and I went hard,
but she grabbed my hand and used that, moaning...
She told me her name on the towpath, holding the fish
in a small sack of water. We walked away from the lights.
She'd come too far with me now. She looked back, once.

A town like this would kill me. A gypsy read my palm.
She saw fame. I could be anything with my looks,
my luck, my brains. I bought a guitar and blew a smoke ring
at the moon. Elvis nothing. *I'm not that type,* she said.
Too late. I eased her down by the dull canal
and talked sexy. Useless. She stared at the goldfish, silent.
I grabbed the plastic bag. She cried as it gasped and wriggled
on the grass and here we are. A dog craps by a lamp post.

Mama, straight up, I hope you rot in hell. The old man
sloped off, sharpish. I saw her through the kitchen window.
The sky slammed down on my school cap, chicken licken.
Lady, Sweetheart, Princess I say now, but I never stay.
My sandwiches were near her thigh, then the Rent Man
lit her cigarette and I ran, ran... She is in the canal.
These streets are quiet, as if the town has held its breath
to watch the Wheel go round above the dreary homes.

No, don't. Imagine. One thump did it, then I was on her,
giving her everything I had. Jack the Lad, Ladies' Man.
Easier to say Yes. Easier to stay a child, wide-eyed
at the top of the helter-skelter. You get one chance in this life
and if you screw it you're done for, uncle, no mistake.
She lost a tooth. I picked her up, dead slim, and slid her in.
A girl like that should have a paid-up solitaire and high hopes,
but she asked for it. A right-well knackered outragement.

My reflection sucks a sour Woodbine and buys me a drink.
    Here's
looking at you. Deep down I'm talented. She found out. Don't
    mess
with me, angel, I'm no nutter. Over in the corner, a dead ringer
for Ruth Ellis smears a farewell kiss on the lip of a gin-and-lime.
The barman calls Time. Bang in the centre of my skull,
there's a strange coolness. I could almost fly. Tomorrow
will find me elsewhere, with a loss of memory. Drink up son,
the world's your fucking oyster. Awopbopaloobop alopbimbam.

EVERY GOOD BOY

I put this breve down, knowing in my head
the sound it makes before I play a note.
C sharp is D flat, changing if I place it here,
or here, or there. Listen. I mostly use a minor key.

These days, the world lacks harmony. The inner cities
riot in my inner ear. *Discord*, say the critics,
but that is what I hear; even in this quiet room
where I deploy blatant consecutive fifths, a hooligan.

That time I was mugged, I came back here
and sat for hours in silence. I have only ever wanted
to compose. The world strikes me and I make
my sound. I make no claim to greatness.

If they were caught, I would like half an hour
together, to show how this phrase, here, excites;
how the smash of broken glass is turned
into a new motif. I would like to share that with them.

YES, OFFICER

It was about the time of day you mention, yes.
I remember noticing the quality of light
beyond the bridge. I lit a cigarette.

I saw some birds. I knew the words for them
and their collective noun. A skein of geese. This cell
is further away from anywhere I've ever been. Perhaps.

I was in love. *For God's sake, don't.*
Fear is the first taste of blood in a dry mouth.
I have no alibi. Yes, I used to have a beard.

No, no. I wouldn't use that phrase. The more you ask
the less I have to say. There was a woman crying
on the towpath, dressed in grey. *Please.* Sir.

Without my own language, I am a blind man
in the wrong house. Here come the fists, the boots.
I curl in a corner, uttering empty vowels until

they have their truth. That is my full name.
With my good arm I sign a forgery. Yes, Officer,
I did. I did and these, your words, admit it.

STATEMENT

It happened like this. I shall never forget. Da
was drunk again, came in from the yard
with his clenched face like a big fist, leaving
the back door open... that low moon, full
and dangerous, at the end of the close. *Jesus Christ,*
he said, *I'd be better dead,* picked up the old clock
from the mantelpiece and flung it on the fire.

It burned till morning came. He kept her up
all night, shouting the bad bits over again
till she put her head in her hands and wept.
Her apron was a map of Ireland. He jabbed
his finger to the North, bruising her breast, yelled
There! There! God's truth, she tried to kiss him,
though Tom's near 21 and that was the last time.

Then she starts... *In the warfare against the devil,*
the world, and the flesh, on whom must we depend?...
and he's ripped the floorboard up. No chance. Her face
was at the window when they got him, watching him
dance for the Queen's men, sweating blood
doing it. I came running down, said *Mammy,*
Mammy, and she turned with her arms like the crucifix.

MONEY TALKS

I am the authentic language of suffering. My cold, gold eye
does not blink. Mister, you want nice time? No problem.
I say *Screw You*. I buy and sell the world. I got
Midas touch, turn bread to hard cash. My million tills
sing through the night, my shining mad machines.
I stink and accumulate. Do you fancy me, lady? Really?

See me pass through the eye of a needle! Whoopee,
I cut Time dead with my sleek facelift. I travel
faster than $-sound. Don't give me away; after all, no one
can eat me. Honey, I'm a jealous God, $-stammering
my one commandment on the calculator. *Love me*.
Under your fingernails I smile up with my black grin.

Don't let my oily manner bother you, Sir, I'll get you
a taxi, get you a limousine. I know a place
where it's raining dollar bills. I got any currency
you want, women and gigolos, metal tuxedos. The party
is one long gold-toothed scream. Have a good day. I am
the big bombs, sighing in their thick lead sheaths OK.

SELLING MANHATTAN

All yours, Injun, twenty-four bucks' worth of glass beads,
gaudy cloth. I got myself a bargain. I brandish
fire-arms and fire-water. Praise the Lord.
Now get your red ass out of here.

I wonder if the ground has anything to say.
You have made me drunk, drowned out
the world's slow truth with rapid lies.
But today I hear again and plainly see. Wherever
you have touched the earth, the earth is sore.

I wonder if the spirit of the water has anything
to say. That you will poison it. That you
can no more own the rivers and the grass than own
the air. I sing with true love for the land;
dawn chant, the song of sunset, starlight psalm.

Trust your dreams. No good will come of this.
My heart is on the ground, as when my loved one
fell back in my arms and died. I have learned
the solemn laws of joy and sorrow, in the distance
between morning's frost and firefly's flash at night.

Man who fears death, how many acres do you need
to lengthen your shadow under the endless sky?
Last time, this moment, now, a boy feels his freedom
vanish, like the salmon going mysteriously
out to sea. Loss holds the silence of great stones.

I will live in the ghost of grasshopper and buffalo.

The evening trembles and is sad.
A little shadow runs across the grass
and disappears into the darkening pines.

POLITICO

Corner of Thistle Street, two slack shillings jangled
in his pocket. Wee Frank. Politico. A word in the right
got things moving. *A free beer for they dockers
and the guns will come through in the morning. No bother.*

Bread rolls and Heavy came up the rope to the window
where he and McShane were making a stand. *Someone
sent up a megaphone, for Christ's sake.* Occupation.
Aye. And the soldiers below just biding their time.

Blacklisted. Bar L. *That scunner, Churchill.* The Clyde
where men cheered theirselves out of work as champagne
butted a new ship. Spikes at the back of the toilet seat.
Alls I'm doing is fighting for wur dignity. Away.

*Smoke-filled rooms? Wait till I tell you... Listen,
I'm ten years dead and turning in my urn. Socialism?
These days?* There's the tree that never grew. *Och,
a shower of shites.* There's the bird that never flew.

SCRAPS

That Thursday, it seemed they were part of the rain,
a drizzling chain,
men and women, colourless,
stretching down Renshaw Street.

This was a B movie,
grainy black-and-white,
with *Buddy, Can You Spare A Dime*
thin on the soundtrack.

Breeze from the river
scuffed litter round their shoes,
one scrap an old pound note
no one could spend.

A cat pissed on the steps of Renshaw Hall.

Scraps. Scraps. Scraps of language
mashed in a scum
above the sluggish drains.

There's nothing down for us.
Enough to make you be a bloody copper.
What's the time?

UB40. Giro.
Words had died a death.
DHSS.

Under the dripping phone wires
under the slumping clouds
a stunted man went down the line.
Help on a rusty harmonica
snagged by the wind.

And overhead
the seagulls
calling their bleak farewells to the old ships.
Nowhere to go, nothing to do
but circle the city's black grooves,
repeating its past like a scratched LP.

Nobody's famous
here and now.
The cracks in the cathedral widen.
Kids chase dragons through the drab estates,
accomplished fire-eaters.

All My Loving. Three feet from the ground
his face peered up.
You must be joking, pal.
Everybody's breath fumed in the air.

Cats and dogs.
The line moved on.

A woman threw a silver shilling at a dwarf.

STEALING

The most unusual thing I ever stole? A snowman.
Midnight. He looked magnificent; a tall, white mute
beneath the winter moon. I wanted him, a mate
with a mind as cold as the slice of ice
within my own brain. I started with the head.

Better off dead than giving in, not taking
what you want. He weighed a ton; his torso,
frozen stiff, hugged to my chest, a fierce chill
piercing my gut. Part of the thrill was knowing
that children would cry in the morning. Life's tough.

Sometimes I steal things I don't need. I joy-ride cars
to nowhere, break into houses just to have a look.
I'm a mucky ghost, leave a mess, maybe pinch a camera.
I watch my gloved hand twisting the doorknob.
A stranger's bedroom. Mirrors. I sigh like this – *Aah.*

It took some time. Reassembled in the yard,
he didn't look the same. I took a run
and booted him. Again. Again. My breath ripped out
in rags. It seems daft now. Then I was standing
alone amongst lumps of snow, sick of the world.

Boredom. Mostly I'm so bored I could eat myself.
One time, I stole a guitar and thought I might
learn to play. I nicked a bust of Shakespeare once,
flogged it, but the snowman was strangest.
You don't understand a word I'm saying, do you?

TRANSLATION

(*All writing is garbage* – ARTAUD)

She wore gloves, red to the elbow, sipped
at a dry martini, dry-eyed, said *I have come
to confess. Do you want my love?* The old cathedral
exploded into bells, scattering gulls at the sky
like confetti. But no wedding. Then? The hunchback
swung on the one-armed bandit, slack eyes following
bright uneatable fruit, cranking *Bugger bugger bugger*
from stale breath. Later she held a dun root
on a scarlet palm, real satin, her lover's eyes
dark as a bell-tower, mouth bruising *O O* on the night.
When he pushed into her it was the gambler, crippled,
she invented. Lick me from the navel outwards
darkly in damp circles tell me strange half-truths
from your strange mind babe babe baby.

COLOURS BY SOMEONE ELSE

Sweetheart, this evening your smell is all around
down by the fishing-boats, the sky trembling

above the pier. Your tears have dried on my palms.
Darling, we should never have done that.

You made me your own, painted my face
into smithereens. Who can say where my tongue

has been in your dark boudoir? Soft heelprints
on my shoulder, sound of the hummingbird breathing its last.

Regret is in the air. Dante Gabriel Rossetti
saved his poems from her worms. Long hours

turning the rain to whisky. Weeping spectacles.
The landlord sees me mime Sinatra at the bar.

Sweetheart, are you listening? Pay heed
for I am insane on the underground, burning

the crossword with my eyes. I owe money
to a bowler hat, keep a brick from London Bridge

under the bed. We are drowning twice nightly
in rivers of silk. This is the Year of the Tiger.

Hush. There is no end to my love for you, for I
have eaten the owl's egg, endured the sharpening of spoons.

When you see me in my uniform, act unconcerned.
The pin and pomegranate will suffice to show

the workings of my mind. I am up to my eyes
in onions. Sweetheart. Undress and read this.

THREE PAINTINGS

I THE ONE-EYED FLAUTIST PLAYS FOR THE PRINCE

Minims have one eye, crotchets, breves... quavers wink
with a quick wit. My one eye sees this, my good eye
can shape the invisible from inked-in rosaries.
For the glory of God's blind angels, liquid pearls.

So. You find me difficult. Your gaze drops
to the floor, you fumble awkwardly. I pause, staring,
notice your mistress, Highness, edge from the scene,
though her own ghost rustles on my darker side.

Stuff your discomfiture. I cover my flute's six eyes
till they fill with dreams beyond this brief audition.
I am only a moment away from bliss, the note
which almost bestows a kiss you cannot imagine.

As for the rest, call it unfortunate. Her punishment
was worse, whose sweet face then is locked forever
in my inner eye. I would suffer as much today
to see her see me whole. Now let me play.

He spoke early. Not the *goo goo goo* of infancy,
but *I am God.* Joseph kept away, carving himself
a silent Pinocchio out in the workshed. He said
he was a simple man and hadn't dreamed of this.

She grew anxious in that second year, would stare
at stars saying *Gabriel? Gabriel?* Your guess.
The village gossiped in the sun. The child was solitary,
his wide and solemn eyes could fill your head.

After he walked, our normal children crawled. Our wives
were first resentful, then superior. Mary's child
would bring her sorrow... better far to have a son
who gurgled nonsense at your breast. *Googoo. Googoo.*

But I am God. We heard him through the window,
heard the smacks which made us peep. What we saw
was commonplace enough. But afterwards, we wondered
why the infant did not cry. And why the Mother did.

3 JANE AVRIL DANCING

What you staring at? Buy me a bleeding drink! Jane Avril
yelled in rough red French for more wine, her mind
in a pool on the table. She had seen better days.

Me, I thought her lovely still. I am a man susceptible
to beauty. Sometimes she sang to her own reflection.
Some love song. Even her dress seemed grubbily sad.

...sweetest lips, I want to taste you,
something la la la embrace you...

But I had my own problems, that winter of absinthe,
impotence, Paris empty and the bitch off with Dufy.
I loved her almost as much as she thought I did.

Jane was a pale motif on darker shades, and I
a shadow of my former self, when she returned.
She gave me a flower and whispered *Love me. Darling.*

What is joy? I keep the petals. She promised everything
that afternoon, though what I remember now is the look
which only she could throw and *la la la* Jane Avril, dancing.

MOUTH, WITH SOAP

She didn't shit, she *soiled* or *had a soil*
and didn't piss, *passed water*. Saturday night,
when the neighbours were fucking, she *submitted*
to intercourse and, though she didn't sweat cobs then,
later she *perspired*. Jesus wept. Bloody Nora. *Language!*

She was a deadly assassin as far as
words went. Slit-eyed, thin-lipped, she
bleached and boiled the world. No Fs or Cs,
Ps and Qs minded, oh aye. She did not bleed,
had *Women's Trouble* locked in the small room, mutely.

In the beginning was The Word and, close behind,
The Censor, clacking a wooden tongue. Watch out
for the tight vocabulary of living death. *Wash out*
your mouth with soap. She hoovered on Sundays, always,
a constant drizzle in her heart; below it *The Big C*, growing.

BIG SUE AND *NOW VOYAGER*

Her face is a perfect miniature on wide, smooth flesh,
a tiny fossil in a slab of stone. Most evenings
Big Sue is Bette Davis. Alone. The curtains drawn.
The TV set an empty head which has the same
recurring dream. Mushrooms taste of kisses. Sherry trifle
is a honeymoon. *Be honest. Who'd love me?*

Paul Henreid. He lights two cigarettes and, gently,
puts one in her mouth. The little flat in Tooting
is a floating ship. Violins. Big Sue drawing deeply
on a chocolate stick. *Now Voyager depart. Much,*
much for thee is yet in store. Her eyes are wider,
bright. The previous video unspools the sea.

This is where she lives, the wrong side of the glass
in black-and-white. To press the rewind,
replay, is to know perfection. Certainty. The soundtrack
drowns out daytime echoes. *Size of her. Great cow.*
Love is never distanced into memory, persists
unchanged. Oscar-winners looking at the sky.

Why wish for the moon? Outside the window night falls,
slender women rush to meet their dates. Men whistle
on the dark blue streets at shapes they want
or, in the pubs, light cigarettes for two. Big Sue
unwraps a Mars Bar, crying at her favourite scene.
The bit where Bette Davis says *We have the stars.*

ALL DAYS LOST DAYS

Living
in and out of the past,
inexplicably
so many things have died
in me.

In and out like a tide,
each tear
holds a tiny hologram.
Even this early
I am full of years.

Here are the little gravestones
where memory
stands in the wild grass,
watching the future
arrive in a line of big black cars.

All days
lost days, in and out of themselves
between dreaming
and dreaming again and half-
remembering.

FOREIGN

Imagine living in a strange, dark city for twenty years.
There are some dismal dwellings on the east side
and one of them is yours. On the landing, you hear
your foreign accent echo down the stairs. You think
in a language of your own and talk in theirs.

Then you are writing home. The voice in your head
recites the letter in a local dialect; behind that
is the sound of your mother singing to you,
all that time ago, and now you do not know
why your eyes are watering and what's the word for this.

You use the public transport. Work. Sleep. Imagine one night
you saw a name for yourself sprayed in red
against a brick wall. A hate name. Red like blood.
It is snowing on the streets, under the neon lights,
as if this place were coming to bits before your eyes.

And in the delicatessen, from time to time, the coins
in your palm will not translate. Inarticulate,
because this is not home, you point at fruit. Imagine
that one of you says *Me not know what these people mean.*
It like they only go to bed and dream. Imagine that.

POSTCARDS

It was a courtship of postcards
which linked the love in London
to the love in Lancashire, franking-machines
pressing their ink kisses
over her name.

She was adored
by the sender of Renoir's summer women,
Grimshaw's rainy streets,
the Clouseau fan against the Beumb.
I miss you, L.

Some days the weather
had been moved to tears
by landscape,
like the view from Heptonstall,
blurring the words.

My Darling... when...

Or she laughed at the moustache
upon the Mona Lisa,
kept Mae West a week
upon the mantelpiece
asking her up.

A white card
with A Hole to See the Sky Through,
nothing else, arrived
and, mirror-written on the back,
.THƆINOT ƎM ƎNOHꟼ

Three words in a thought bubble
from Chairman Mao
reiterated Ronald Reagan's words
once more with feeling. Even
Thatcher loved her.

O'Keefe. Picasso. Donald McGill.
The last one
was a photograph of Rodin's Kiss,
without a stamp
and wishing she were here.

CORRESPONDENTS

When you come on Thursday, bring me a letter. We have
the language of stuffed birds, teacups. We don't have
the language of bodies. My husband will be here.
I shall inquire after your wife, stirring his cup
with a thin spoon and my hand shall not tremble.
Give me the letter as I take your hat. Mention
the cold weather. My skin burns at the sight of you.

We skim the surface, gossip. I baked this cake and you
eat it. Words come from nowhere, drift off
like the smoke from his pipe. Beneath my dress, my breasts
swell for your lips, belly churns to be stilled
by your brown hands. This secret life is Gulliver,
held down by strings of pleasantries. I ache. Later
your letter flares up in the heat and is gone.

Dearest Beloved, pretend I am with you... I read
your dark words and do to myself things
you can only imagine. I hardly know myself.
Your soft, white body in my arms... When we part,
you kiss my hand, bow from the waist, all passion
patiently restrained. *Your servant, Ma'am.* Now you write
wild phrases of love. The words blur as I cry out once.

Next time we meet, in drawing-room or garden,
passing our letters cautiously between us, our eyes
fixed carefully on legal love, think of me here
on my marriage-bed an hour after you've left.
I have called your name over and over in my head
at the point your fiction brings me to. I have kissed
your sweet name on the paper as I knelt by the fire.

TELEGRAMS

URGENT WHEN WE MEET COMPLETE STRANGERS DEAR STOP
THOUGH I COUNT THE HOURS TILL YOU ARE NEAR STOP
WILL EXPLAIN LATER DATE TILL THEN CANT WAIT STOP C

COMPLETELY FOGGED WHAT DO YOU MEAN BABY? STOP
CANT WE SLOPE OFF TO MY PLACE MAYBE? STOP
NOT POSS ACT NOT MET WITH RAISON DETRE STOP B

FOR GODS SAKE JUST TRUST ME SWEETHEART STOP
NATCH IT HURTS ME TOO WHEN WERE APART STOP
SHIT WILL HIT FAN UNLESS STICK TO PLAN STOP C

SHIT? FAN? TRUST? WHATS GOING ON HONEY? STOP
IF THIS IS A JOKE IT ISNT FUNNY STOP
INSIST ON TRUTH LOVE YOU BUT STRUTH! STOP B

YES I KNOW DARLING I LOVE YOU TOO STOP
TRY TO SEE PREDIC FROM MY POINT OF VIEW STOP
IF YOU DONT PLAY BALL I WONT COME AT ALL STOP C

PLEASE REPLY LAST TELEGRAM STOP
HAVE YOU FORGOTTEN THAT NIGHT IN MATLOCK? C

NO WAS TRYING TO TEACH YOU LESSON PET STOP
ALSO BECAUSE OF THESE AM IN DEBT STOP
TRUST WHEN NEXT MEET WILL PASSIONATELY GREET STOP B

NO NO NO NO GET IT THROUGH YOUR THICK HEAD STOP
IF SEEN WITH YOU AM AS GOOD AS DEAD STOP
THE WIFE WILL GUESS WEVE BEEN HAVING SEX STOP C

SO YOURE MARRIED? HA! I MIGHT HAVE GUESSED STOP
THOUGHT IT ODD YOU WORE STRING VEST STOP
AS SOON AS I MET YOU I WENT OVER THE TOP
NOW DO ME A FAVOUR PLEASE PLEASE STOP STOP B

TELEPHONING HOME

I hear your voice saying *Hello* in that guarded way
you have, as if you fear bad news, imagine you
standing in our dark hall, waiting, as my silver coin
jams in the slot and frantic bleeps repeat themselves
along the line until your end goes slack. The wet platform
stretches away from me towards the South and home.

I try again, dial the nine numbers you wrote once
on a postcard. The stranger waiting outside stares
through the glass that isn't there, a sad portrait
someone abandoned. I close my eyes... *Hello?*... see myself
later this evening, two hundred miles and two hours nearer
where I want to be. *I love you.* This is me speaking.

SPACE, SPACE

1 SEARCHING FOR MOONS

There is something to be said but I, for one,
forget. That star went out more years ago
than we can count. Its ghosts see dinosaurs.

The brain says *No* to the Universe, *Prove it*,
but the heart is susceptible, pining for a look,
a kind word. Some are brought to their knees,

pleading in dead language at a deaf ear. Spaceships
float in nothing in the dark, searching for moons
to worship with their fish eyes. It must be love.

2 ASTRONOMER

In love with space, stares up
as breath smokes signals into night.
Light years, loneliness, dark waves

lapping moons. From there sees absences,
gone worlds; from here perceives
new galaxies where nowhere is.

LOVESICK

I found an apple.
A red and shining apple.
I took its photograph.

I hid the apple in the attic.
I opened the skylight
and the sun said *Ah!*

At night, I checked that it was safe,
under the giggling stars,
the sly moon. My cool apple.

Whatever you are calling about,
I am not interested.
Go away. You with the big teeth.

STRANGE PLACE

I watch you undress by household candlelight.
We are having an early night. On the wireless
news from other countries half distracts me.

Each small movement makes a longer shadow
on the wall. I lie here quietly as garments fall.
A faint voice talks of weather somewhere else.

But we are here and now, listening to nothing blindly,
where there is no news or weather. Love, later,
I will feel homesick for this strange place.

ONLY DREAMING

A ghost loves you, has got inside you in the dark.
Whose face does he wear? He changes his features
all night whilst you tell yourself you're dreaming,
only dreaming, but he puts his tongue in your mouth.
Yes, you say in your sleep to nothing, *Darling*.
He wears a dead face, a woman's face, you fold
into yourself and feel her breasts, talk gibberish.

You tell no one of this unfaithfulness in the small hours.
The ghost is devoted, stares into your eyes behind the lids.
This is the real thing. He has turned your face
to the pillow, mouth open, breathing his warm breath
for him. Name him. Say it. Come on, c'mon.
Your hands grasp him, pass straight through, wake you
touching yourself, crying aloud into the room. Abandoned.

BY HEART

I made myself imagine that I didn't love you,
that your face was ordinary to me. This was in our house
when you were out, secret, guessing what such difference

would be like, never to have known your touch,
your taste. Then I went out and passed the places
where we'd go, without you there, pretending that I could.

Making believe I could, I tried to blot out longing,
or regret, when someone looked like you, head down,
laughing, running away from me behind a veil of rain.

So it was strange to see you, just ahead of me,
as I trailed up the hill, thinking how I can't unlearn
the words I've got by heart, or dream your name away,

and shouting it, involuntarily, three times, until
you turned and smiled. Love makes buildings home
and out of dreary weather, sometimes, rainbows come.

WARMING HER PEARLS

for Judith Radstone

Next to my own skin, her pearls. My mistress
bids me wear them, warm them, until evening
when I'll brush her hair. At six, I place them
round her cool, white throat. All day I think of her,

resting in the Yellow Room, contemplating silk
or taffeta, which gown tonight? She fans herself
whilst I work willingly, my slow heat entering
each pearl. Slack on my neck, her rope.

She's beautiful. I dream about her
in my attic bed; picture her dancing
with tall men, puzzled by my faint, persistent scent
beneath her French perfume, her milky stones.

I dust her shoulders with a rabbit's foot,
watch the soft blush seep through her skin
like an indolent sigh. In her looking-glass
my red lips part as though I want to speak.

Full moon. Her carriage brings her home. I see
her every movement in my head.... Undressing,
taking off her jewels, her slim hand reaching
for the case, slipping naked into bed, the way

she always does.... And I lie here awake,
knowing the pearls are cooling even now
in the room where my mistress sleeps. All night
I feel their absence and I burn.

DEPORTATION

They have not been kind here. Now I must leave,
the words I've learned for supplication,
gratitude, will go unused. Love is a look
in the eyes in any language, but not here,
not this year. They have not been welcoming.

I used to think the world was where we lived
in space, one country shining in big dark.
I saw a photograph when I was small.

Now I am *Alien*. Where I come from there are few jobs,
the young are sullen and do not dream. My lover
bears our child and I was to work here, find
a home. In twenty years we would say This is you
when you were a baby, when the plum tree was a shoot...

We will tire each other out, making our homes
in one another's arms. We are not strong enough.

They are polite, recite official jargon endlessly.
Form F. Room 12. Box 6. I have felt less small
below mountains disappearing into cloud
than entering the Building of Exile. Hearse taxis
crawl the drizzling streets towards the terminal.

I am no one special. An ocean parts me from my love.

Go back. She will embrace me, ask what it was like.
Return. One thing – there was a space to write
the colour of her eyes. They have an apple here,
a bitter-sweet, which matches them exactly. Dearest,
without you I am nowhere. It was cold.

PLAINSONG

Stop. Along this path, in phrases of light,
trees sing their leaves. No Midas touch
has turned the wood to gold, late in the year
when you pass by, suddenly sad, straining
to remember something you're sure you knew.

Listening. The words you have for things die
in your heart, but grasses are plainsong,
patiently chanting the circles you cannot repeat
or understand. This is your homeland,
Lost One, Stranger who speaks with tears.

It is almost impossible to be here and yet
you kneel, no one's child, absolved by late sun
through the branches of a wood, distantly
the evening bell reminding you, *Home, Home,*
Home, and the stone in your palm telling the time.

MILES AWAY

I want you and you are not here. I pause
in this garden, breathing the colour thought is
before language into still air. Even your name
is a pale ghost and, though I exhale it again
and again, it will not stay with me. Tonight
I make you up, imagine you, your movements clearer
than the words I have you say you said before.

Wherever you are now, inside my head you fix me
with a look, standing here whilst cool late light
dissolves into the earth. I have got your mouth wrong,
but still it smiles. I hold you closer, miles away,
inventing love, until the calls of nightjars
interrupt and turn what was to come, was certain,
into memory. The stars are filming us for no one.

Other books by Carol Ann Duffy

STANDING FEMALE NUDE

'... a book that marks the debut of a genuine and original poet'
– ROBERT NYE, *The Times*

'Carol Ann Duffy is a very pure poet... It is good to see a crusading sensibility refusing to surrender any touch of art to the urgency of its cause' – PETER PORTER, *Observer*

THE OTHER COUNTRY

'*The Other Country* is a slim volume like few that have been published recently: urgent, packed with future classics – a book that proclaims that poetry is alive' – PETER FORBES, *Guardian*

'It voices political-erotic challenge, always knows where it's going, and has serious fun on the way' – RUTH PADEL, *Times Literary Supplement*

MEAN TIME

'Carol Ann Duffy is one of the freshest and bravest talents to emerge in British poetry – any poetry – for years'
– EAVAN BOLAND, *Independent on Sunday*

'*Mean Time*... maintains the standards of its predecessors, and may, in fact, surpass them in its treatment of love and memory... to have something to add on these matters, and to deliver it with such force and economy, indicates gifts of a high order' – SEAN O'BRIEN, *Sunday Times*

Mean Time received the Forward Poetry Prize and the Whitbread Poetry Award for 1993.

ANVIL NEW POETS 2 (ed.)

Selections from the work of nine new poets, chosen and introduced by Carol Ann Duffy. The poets are: Sean Boustead, Colette Bryce, Kate Clanchy, Oliver Comins, Christina Dunhill, Alice Oswald, Richard Price, Mike Venner and John Whale. 'The first collections of all these writers should be worth looking forward to' – *Times Literary Supplement*

New and Recent Poetry from Anvil

TONY CONNOR
Metamorphic Adventures

PETER DALE
Edge to Edge
SELECTED POEMS

DICK DAVIS
Touchwood

DICK DAVIS
Borrowed Ware
MEDIEVAL PERSIAN EPIGRAMS

MICHAEL HAMBURGER
Collected Poems 1941–1994

JAMES HARPUR
The Monk's Dream

ANTHONY HOWELL
First Time in Japan

PETER LEVI
Reed Music

CHARLES MADGE
Of Love, Time and Places
SELECTED POEMS

E. A. MARKHAM
Misapprehensions

THOMAS McCARTHY
The Lost Province

PETER RUSSELL
The Elegies of Quintilius

PHILIP SHERRARD
In the Sign of the Rainbow
SELECTED POEMS 1940–1989

RUTH SILCOCK
A Wonderful View of the Sea

A catalogue of our publications is available on request

The
Abandoned
Puppy
and other tales

Holly Webb
Illustrated by Sophy Williams

LiTTLE TiGER
LONDON

Other titles by Holly Webb